Happy 30th

Chainsaws In The Cathedral

For Dean
Hope you enjoy these poems. It was easier writing them than living them. Keep well.
Peter

Books by Peter Trower

Poetry

Poems for a Dark Sunday (mimeo)
Moving Through the Mystery
Between the Sky and the Splinters
The Alders and Others
Ragged Horizons
Bush Poems
Goosequill Snags
The Slidingback Hills
Unmarked Doorways
Where Roads Lead
Hitting the Bricks
Chainsaws in the Cathedral

Prose

Rough and Ready Times
Grogan's Cafe (novel)
Dead Man's Ticket (novel)

Chainsaws in the Cathedral

Collected Woods Poems
1964 - 1998

Peter Trower

Ekstasis Editions

Canadian Cataloguing in Publication Data

Trower, Peter,
    Chainsaws in the cathedral

    Poems
    ISBN 1-896860-46-X

        1. Trower, Peter, 1930--Poetry.   I. Title.
    Ps8589.R694C5   1999   C811'.54   C99-910352-0
    PR9199.3T76C5   1999

© Peter Trower, 1999.
All rights reserved.
Cover Art: Bus Griffiths

Acknowledgements:
Some of these poems originally appeared in: *Moving Through the Mystery; Between the Sky and the Splinters; The Alders and Others; Ragged Horizons; Bush Poems; Goosequill Snags; Un marked Doorways; The Slidingback Hills; Where Roads Lead; Business Logger; Vancouver; Western Living; B.C. Bookworld; The Sunshine Coast News* and *Raincoast Chronicles.*

Published in 1999 by:
Ekstasis Editions Canada Ltd.   Ekstasis Editions
Box 8474, Main Postal Outlet   Box 571
Victoria, B.C. V8W 3S1   Banff, Alberta T0L 0C0

The Canada Council | Le Conseil des Arts
For the Arts | du Canada
Since 1957 | Depuis 1957

Chainsaws in the Cathedral: Collected Woods Poem has been published with the assistance of a grant from the Canada Council and the Cultural Services Branch of British Columbia.

Contents

Author's Foreward	9
Introduction by Al Purdy	10
Prologue	13
Northflight over Wilderness	15
The Doing	17
A Ticket to Ramsay Arm	19
Lowest-Paid Job in the Woods	20
Steampot	22
Blowdown	24
The Fog Loggers	26
In the Gully	28
Lightning Rod	30
Spar-Tree Raising	32
Early Shift	34
A Wild Girl to Walk the Weathers With	35
The Beacons of the Bad Days	36
Like a War	38
Under Fire	40
Booby Trap	42
Day to Day Blues	44
Goliath Country	45
Sidehill Dentistry	46
And Hell, He Makes Me Laugh	47
Joshua	49
The Trackers	51
The Snow Sadness of January	53
Cinderwind	54
Waterbomber	56
Mexican Standoff	57
Trackloader	59
The Finishing	61
Skookumchuck	62

The Animals	63
Grease for the Wheels of Winter	65
The Dead	66
The Ridge Trees	68

The Remembering — 69

A Testament of Hills	71
Hoodoo Cove	77
A Man Gone Mad with Logging	79
Ghostcamp	81
Logger's Rain	83
Ghosts Have No Money to Spend	85
Elephants's Graveyard	87
The Faller's Story	88
Chainsaws in the Cathedral	90
The Old Campaign	91
The Mountains; The Valley	93
The Poem Rower	96
Dream Shift	97
A Crooked Coliseum for the Wind	98
The Slidingback Hills	99
The Last Spar-Tree on Elphinstone Mountain	100
A Mountain Shudders Through Me	102
The Alders	104

The Legends — 105

The King of Rhymes and Whistles	107
Bullpuncher	108
The Country of the Bull	110
Grandaddy Tough	112
Logger Hunt	114
Truckjammer	117
Tombstone on Goatfoot Mountain	119
Goosequill Snags	122
The Last Handfallers	124
Collision Course	126
Running Scared with the Sky-Hanger	128
Horsefly Harry	130

Old Hooker Bill	132
The Song	133
Between the Sky and the Splinters	136
The Ravens	138
Epilogue	141
Grapple Yarder	143
Glossary of Logging Terms	145

Author's Foreword

Chainsaws in the Cathedral (the title was suggested by Al Purdy) represents my entire output of publishable logging poetry to date. I have included only material that deals directly with the arduous business of falling timber and getting it from the woods to the water. Peripheral work that merely deals with the outdoors in a general way or with other activities such as surveying, can be found in other collections.

The poems here have been divided into three categories plus a prologue, epilogue and glossary. The first section *'The Doing'* concentrates on poems of direct experience—the warts-and-all business of actually being a logger. *'The Remembering'* contains poems of reflection—a career logger looking back across the sidehills of his past. The final grouping *'The Legends'* deals with specific characters who, for one reason or another, stick firmly in the memory. It also contains a couple of logger fantasies.

The book contains fifteen poems that have not previously seen print. The rest, many of them from long-unavailable books have been revised, some extensively. The collection's ultimate aim is to present a realistic and well-rounded picture of what it was like to be a westcoast logger in the Forties, Fifties, Sixties and Seventies.

Peter Trower
Gibsons, B.C.
1998

Dedication

To Robert Swanson who lit the spark in me, years back; to my great friend Al Purdy, whose support and encouragement kept it burning, to my old logger pal, Bus Griffiths, fellow custodian of the legends and to Yvonne who changed my life and still walks the weathers with me.

Peter Trower

Introduction

by Al Purdy

There is no one who writes like Peter Trower. And now I have to say how he writes, which isn't very easy.

All right then—: Pete's words jump and push and leap and whisper and roar in your ears. All the strange jargon of loggers is at his command. Sometimes he uses rhyme and metre, but more often it's bounding careening free verse. Sometimes ten dollar educated words, then woods jargon that snaps and crackles in the ears.

They're enjoyable, these poems, that's what I want to emphasize most. Influences? Trower has been likened to Robert Swanson, but that's libel. Pete Trower is a poet who writes logging poems; Swanson was a logger who wrote doggerel. I do not intend to demean Swanson, even if it sounds like it. But Swanson was just not in Trower's class; as Robert Service could not be compared to Kipling.

Trower's overt subject matter in this book is, of course, logging and the lives of the men who follow that trade. But there are many other themes. British Columbia's forests are gradually and swiftly disappearing as the chainsaw whine shrieks to a crescendo. There is sadness and nostalgia for the great trees; also for a way of life that he, Trower, experienced and both loved and hated.

Beyond logging, there is life itself, the winning and losing, loving and hating; blood running among the words; sweat greasing commas and periods. And Wow, the way that Pete handles words. They jump through hoops for him, turn somersaults and even seem to arm wrestle with each other. Undoubtedly that sounds like exaggeration, but it ain't. To make your words resound like bells in your own and a reader's ears is both easy and impossible to do. Easy to write words on a page; but then you deceive yourself if you settle for less than the best you're capable of—and let the 'prepositions dangle where they will.'

So am I prejudiced when writing about Peter Trower? Of course I am. But then his writings were the first thing I ever knew about him. I'm glad to be prejudiced.

Al Purdy, Sidney, B.C., 1998

Prologue

Northflight Over Wilderness

Explosion of terrain
greengray fogfingered desolate
forests beyond feet
heights beyond hands
rainridges beyond reckoning
wild to the horizon

Upland meadowgrass
shawling from hillspines —
clear stare of blue lakes
ice-lashed in lost craters —
hanging rugs of stone
ragged against the sky —
monoliths pyramids dragonbacks —
tablelands windwitched at evening —
stark cones swaddled in cloud —
snow parapets remote in pewter light —
great ramps of scree where the granite gave up

Glacial streams
gouting down gullies —
flashing daggers at the the sun —
gnashing through mountain tunnels —
cataracting over cliffs —
bobsledding down troughs and spillways —
grinding the the rock teeth of riverbeds —
slowing to froth and steel on the flat —
toppling over final land-lips —
becoming ocean

Emerald trees
feathering out forever —
roots splay-fingering
worm-winding in the dirt —
trunks struggling up
through strata of slatted shadow —
crowns drinking the light
wearing the sky,
huge-boled in the valley bottoms —
dwindling to dwarves at the timberline
Shining predatory eagles
still-winged on updrafts —
bear cubs tussling in clearings
drunk with spring —
moose with horns like huge webbed hands
ruminating in undiscovered valleys —
quick-as-a-wink squirrels —
shy ambling porcupines —
fish snapping flies in lazy sloughs —
all your unseen children

Womanland
beware our small shadow
as it omens across your glories —
it is only one of many —
you are under siege —
there is no escape
We are the ones who have never learned
to leave well enough alone
We are the creatures you have no pact with
come to betray you

THE DOING

A Ticket to Ramsay Arm
for Jack Williams

One slackassed spring
I picked up a hiring-slip from a mancatcher in a bar —
told him I'd fly up the following day —
guy was so tickled he fronted me twenty bucks

I had more good intentions than a SallyAnn street preacher
but with all that moolah, I ran a little amok —
found a lot of beer   a bottle   a broad —
missed the goddamn plane

Well, I kicked myself a bit over that one —
played the duck for the mancatcher —
felt like sixteen kinds of a drunken fool
till I read the evening paper

Seems like half a bloody mountain
had slid down on the camp I was bound for —
bulldozed the cookshack into the sea —
buried the rest of it   killed five men

One of those poor stiffs could have been me!
That was about the only time
drinking ever handed me more
than a sore head and a bad reputation.

The Lowest-Paid Job in the Woods

The whistle-punk I was staggers
up muddy hills in a rattle of rain
uncoiling as he climbs
a heavy noose of wire   umbilical lengths
trailing away behind   across the canyon
to the slave-driving mother machine

The rest of the crew's pulling strawline
so nobody's getting off easy
except the engineer
and at least my load lightens
with every black coil
I throw away

Come at last
to a likely vantage-point
I scale a cedar stump and sit
smoking   sweating   swearing
as raindrops bounce from the duck's-back rubber —
I'm wetter than hell anyhow

They're rigged up and it's starting time —
someone shrieks like a goosed owl —
I press the wooden dingus in my fist —
the horn cries —
the engineer hits his levers —
the choked logs leap to life
thrash and batter down the slope
to the spar-tree

Between shouted signals
I dream of songs and stories —
think of the legendary whistle-punk
back in the Dirty Thirties
whose partner was killed on the rigging
by a production-crazy foreman —
who stayed on in camp   waited his chance
caught the foreman in the bight
blew the wrong whistle   let the logs take him
blamed a raven   sailed away
proving vengeance
is not the sole province of heaven

They call me a whistle-punk
I must endure
the stinging tradition of their scorn
when daily I hold their lives   like mice
at the mercy of my fingers.

Steampot

A genuine hunk of history
is dying right here in front of us
snorting out its last
in this frozen westcoast swamp —
bound to contribute its bones
to the floor of the Tahsis Valley —
a refugee from the glory days
sold out to the gas-rigs and diesels

But she's a long way from dead yet
that smoke-puking old relic
She's got a belly full of fog
and she's raring to rampage
Old Sven the woodsplitter
plugs the firebox tight
Shorty, last of the jerkwire punks
trips the steamvalve and whistles her loose

With that wild hoot still shaking the draws
she whirls back her main-drum and reefs
The mainline tightens like God had ahold —
jerks the turn free like peeling bananas
Couple of fatbutt fir logs too —
she bullies them in like matchsticks
Hangups? Hell! She'll tear out the stumps!
power to squander, that battlescarred bastard

But we've small time to study on symbols
We're too busy dodging those fired-back chokers —
trying to light smokes with wet matches   cursing
Captain Cook for finding this country
In the sting of a mean ocean wind
there is little profit in too much thinking —
no time for a sense of history
when a dinosaur whips us to work in its death-throes.

Blowdown

That winter, Typhoon Frieda
hit the coast with a primal howl
like a pilled-up whore on a rampage —
the Lion's Gate Bridge turned cowardly and shook —
booms tore loose   tugs capsized —
breaking powerlines let in blackness —
windows shattered   rafters cracked —
great trees toppled like coldcocked fighters

In a certain mountain valley
her energies pinching stronger
Frieda levelled half a forest
with one unladylike thrust
Like a machine-gunned army
two million feet of wood went over —
huge hemlocks tore loose their roots
groaned and tottered and fell down flat

To that graveyard of jackstrawed giants
three years later we came
to press our luck in that tangle of trees
with their roots like great ragged wheels
We fought the logs through that obstacle course
cursing to gladden the devil —
impossible hangups exhausted our tricks —
chokers snapped like string on the roots

To make matters happier yet
it was stony treacherous slide country
strewn with moss-pelted boulders
huge as the roots and as troublesome
Above us hung the crumbling cliffs
that had flung the rocks down years back
Often fog came thicker than grief
to blind us to boot on that hard claim

We bought more logs than one there
left them trapped for the damp to eat
No mill will butcher that timber
it rots there yet in the valley's throat
Two million feet   a conundrum of wood —
we puzzled it mostly out in the end
Left the rest to ghosts   to God
and the wind that blows when men grow still.

The Fog Loggers

Cold breath of limbo
is on the mountain
locking us
into unreality —
the broken hydra head
of a silhouetted
sapling root
snarls silently
at the ghosts of day

And we
are the ghosts of day
haunting the eight-hour hill —
quarantined from the world
in the queer time

Phantoms of the fogged
and fallen forest
we move by rote
through a rigged labour,
curtained by a gray sea
in which our noises live

The damp dimensions of morning
close eerie fingers
around us —
the sun   the summer
are unreliable rumours

Professional spectres
committed to our calling,
we will spook this amorphous place
above the real world
until the quitting-whistle
rematerializes us
and we retreat downhill
through the startlespread of afternoon
clammily reprieved.

In the Gully

In the dripping gully
the spider-rooted windfall
sucks up under the granite lip
of the overhang   and stops

Thumb the button
of the electric belt-whistle
I wear like a six-shooter
confident the haul-back line
will jerk the jammed wood free
but it doesn't

Go ahead on the mainline again
Cable grinds against stone
to no avail   The windfall
lies locked in the ravine

Glance at my chokermen
They gaze back blankly
Not their problem
Only and incontestably mine

Go ahead once more
The mainline sings to parting point
Hit the whistle again
at the last grating moment

Back slams the windfall
but this time
there is just enough slack
to unhook the choker

Leave it there thankful, thinking
logging's a lot like writing poetry
Mind cables wrench loose the stubborn ideas
sometimes to wedge them
in hopeless canyons
and knowing just when
to blow the whistle and cut them off
is a knack
of no small importance

Lightning Rod

Cannon-rattle of thunder
black clouds knotting
wild wounds of light
breaking the skin of the sky
scared on the mountain summit
too close to the fireworks
Oh, for the life of a logger
stumbling vulnerable
in the cross-sights of a lightning storm
when you're only a few hops from hell
at the best of times
what with blackjacking chokers
and runaway logs

"Maybe they'll shut her down!"
shouts Johnny the chokerman, hopefully
"Maybe," I say   but I know they won't
those wood-greedy bastards
We're bound to crawl this half-bald mountain
in the acetelyne crackle
till 4:30   Oh, for the life
of a logger   I've got nothing better
on my gunbelt hip than a whistle trigger
to shoot down the danger

Yellow steel-spar pokes
into the glowering sky
like a signalling finger   the storm's
dead overhead now, a snarling
electric dragon   "Goddammit!
Why won't they let us go home?"
yells Johnny   We pick up the chokers
start for the logs   Suddenly
God scores a direct hit
on the spar   Raw voltage
comes sizzling down the cables
and then we're sitting on our butts
several feet back in the bushes
with the fading memory
of a mighty wallop

"Hell with this bullshit!
Let's quit!" I say   But somehow
we don't because we owe
too much money or something   Oh
for the life of a logger   The storm
passes   It begins to rain

Spar-Tree Raising

The tree went up at last
and stood like a symbol
against the sky
where we 'd stuck it

It had been a hard tree
an unwilling tree —
it had given us nothing but trouble
in that high shaley landing

Three times we had failed —
the tree lay stubbornly mocking us —
the hooktender rattled off curses —
flung down his hard-hat

It was weary end-of-the-week Friday —
payday in fact —
the tree jeered voicelessly at our efforts
on the windy plateau

We took a smoke break and considered
that it wasn 't really the tree —
the tieup lines were rotten
The sun crashed through the fog

So we tried once more —
put a cat-blade against the base of it
and under the throbbing mainline
the reluctant spar came up

Now it stood like a Gulliver
tethered by guy-lines   compliant at last
and I think we sighed in relief —
had drinks from the water-bag   perhaps joked.

Early Shift

At 4:30 AM
by the ghostly gas-station
a piece of silver paper
wind-scratching across the asphalt
is a noisy insect for the nerves

I wait, unwillingly awake
with only a gutcan   a cigarette
and random thoughts for company
The cops are all asleep with their guns
The town lies ripe for the taking

But I haven't a burglar's belly
I'll help steal trees instead
from a hill that's warming up for me now
By noon that bitch'll be hot enough
to make the devil sweat blood

Across the last stars
three puny cloud-threads crawl
Not a whisper of rain in those timid bastards
They'll scatter like scared dogs
when the haymaker comes up

It's time   Inescapably the crummy
trails its headlights
through the locked village
come to shanghai me once more
to a clockwork mountain.

A Wild Girl To Walk The Weathers With
for Yvonne

On bleak or blistering days
mountain-goating the hard tilting hills
in gaunt ice-carved valleys
slide-scarred
headstoned with the high-notched stumps
of earlier invasions,
I fear no more the dancing deadly rigging
the sudden sidewinding logs
the down-thundering boulders
for life has opened
and I have at last
a wild girl to walk the weathers with

In other camps   valleys   years
I moved in terror
between the lashing lines
and the not-loving
the not-being-loved
burned more deeply than the fear

But though the hazards remain
ubiquitous as ever
they are endurable now
for life has opened
and I have at last
a wild girl to walk the weathers with

The Beacons of the Bad Days

All day cold in the fir-country
under a dirty-laundry sky
we torch the pitchy stumps for warmth —
move from fire to fire
across a winterwhite hill

Boxed in by weather
we flounder through crotch-high snow
shovelling chokerholes —
stumbling clear as the mainline
sucks the logs free and down
to the growling donkey —
hopping on needled feet
to wring out sodden gloves
before the fleeting luxury of the flames

Working too far from one, we light another
wick of defiance against the day,
pawns of a gung-ho hooktender
Tin-pants Andersen, that slavedriver
urging us stubbornly on —
overdoing his job   no let-up even now
Anyone human would shut her down —
slam the lid on this blizzardly valley —
not that production-crazy sonofabitch —
he's out to make a name for himself

Vaguely we dream of jumping the bastard —
sitting him up on a burning fir —
frying his company ass
till he hollers uncle and lets us go home

We've only our fires to sustain us —
our fanciful visions of mutiny
until the final whistle
that will sign our paroles after forever —
let us limp to the trackside
leaving a trail of guttering beacons
warming only our absences under the wind.

Like A War

No bombs explode   no khaki regiments tramp
to battle in a west-coast logging camp
Yet blood can spill upon the forest floor
and logging can be very like a war

We sat aboard a crummy, tension-creased
The fog rose surely from the vanished east
The foreman said — "I've felt this way before
in Italy   it's something like a war"

The hill was dark and filmed with icy slush
We stumbled through the morning-clammy brush
The sky was grey and vague   The air was raw
with winter   and the game was like a war

The rigging clanked and rattled through the mist
The boxing chokers swung at us   and missed
We wrestled with their steel ropes and swore
and grumbled   It was very like a war

Then far above us, shifting timber groaned
The loader's lonely warning whistle moaned
Two dozen logs came crashing down the draw
The guns had sounded   We were   in a war

Our names could well be written on the butts
of that blind downfall   Terror gripped our guts
We shrank behind our stumps beneath the roar
Like hapless soldiers, we were in a war

Cartwheeling down, the wooden missiles rushed,
an avalanche that battered   slammed and crushed
and passed us   And you couldn't ask for more
if you'd been spared by bullets in a war

Foolhardy veterans, we resumed our work
and choked the timber in the morning murk
We'd tasted action now   We knew the score
They paid us for engaging in a war

The logging slash rears weary in the sun
No truce is called no victory ever won
We bear no weapons but the truth is sure
that what we wage is very like a war

Under Fire
A Variant Version

In that fourteen-hundred foot hole
the fog hangs thicker than spit
masking the giddy tilt of the hill —
drowning us blind in murk
Somewhere above, the donkey drums —
the chokers punch through the blur —
a cold fall rain slants down —
we move like fools to our work

I've logged some miserable claims
but this one takes the prize —
rockbluffs steep as an elephant's ass —
runaway roots and boulders
The hooktender's not an eloquent man
but even he is impressed
"This is like World War Two," he says
"We might just as well be soldiers!"

it's around eleven o'clock
when a warning whistle cuts loose
Something comes crashing down through the fog
that sounds like a cattle stampede
"Get hid!" yells the hooker "The pile's took off!"
We dive for the closest stumps
I crouch there almost pissing my pants
too goddamn frightened to breathe

The runaway logs come battering down
with maybe our names on the butts —
a deadly invisible avalanche
picking up speed in the mist
Like a man in a nightmare, I raise my head —
force my eyes to the right
Ten feet away, a thirty-foot fir
goes thundering crazily past

Then all at once it goes silent as death
till we hear the shouts from above
We take a head-count   nobody's hit
it's all the same as before
But as we stumble back to our work
I know the hooker was right
We are mercenaries who carry no guns
and logging is like a war.

Booby Trap

As though two hands held it bending
the small alder curves tight
over the thin creek that goes dry in summer
It is spring   We blunder about
pretending to be fallers
through eleven acres of boggy bottomland

Powersaw's grumbling
Our own grumbling
The crash of that rotten right-of-way timber
No matter which way we undercut them
they keep dropping crooked and counter
No trusting those devious trash-trees

Steady dribble of rain
An argument by the thin creek
I stand back twisting a smoke
He touches the chain to the bowed tree
The tension explodes
It splits like a sprung trap

Fourteen feet
that mulekicking alder barberchairs back —
catches me clean in the crotch —
tears the fly right out of my jeans —
flings me flat on my ass —
vibrates above me dangerously humming

"You okay?" he yells, running over
our minor dissension forgotten
"Guess so" I mutter uncertainly
so close to a eunuch it doesn't bear dwelling on
We are two green fools falling
Around us the woods hiss disappointment.

Day To Day Blues

And there are always
new hills to climb
which are the same damn hill
wearing different men
and wearing them down

Yesterday I worked in rain
with the flu virus
working in me
tore up more territory
to the hollow music of money

Dripped home in the evening
and changed identity
to sniffle in a baronial living room
a most unliterary guest
as they clicked the coloured words

Out in the morning
to blizzard winds and shutdown
Back to a letter from lucky Karen
in faraway Jamaica,
a joint of ganja
and a vicarious mickey
of therapeutic rum

Goliath Country

Birds circle bewildered
in a scathing grey rain
above this field of the fallen
these huge slain
Cawing puzzlement
they sideslip and swoop
The downed giants lie silent
in more than sleep

There has been great havoc here
an enormous slaughtering
Some David has run amok
with a relentless sling
leaving a broken green chaos
an apocalypse of wood
and a new void in the universe
where Goliaths once stood

They will come to remove the bodies
while the echoes still linger
in driven chariots   driven
by the hard ancient hunger
Birds circle bewildered
like men long travelled
who return to find their homes gone
and the town   levelled

Sidehill Dentistry

Left four upper teeth and some blood
on a mountaintop once
having let my guard down
after three suicide shows in a row
The choker nailed me clean
with a sneaky uppercut —
it was like a love tap
from a steel boxing glove

The teeth weren't up to much admittedly —
they would likely have rotted out anyhow
But they were my teeth for all that
and I prefer to decay at my own pace
The doctor who checked me over
said "You were lucky as hell
Had a chokerman in here last week
with half his face caved in!"

When he put it that way
I suppose the doctor was right
Hell, only half an inch closer
I could have been picking up my brains
I thanked the Lord for small mercies
A week later, I had the stumps pulled
got drunk   met a girl   made clumsy love
with gore-smeared lips like Dracula.

And Hell, He Makes Me Laugh
for Denny Smith

And hell, he makes me laugh —
he sees the cosmic joke
beyond this game of hills —
these endless logs we choke
beyond the whipping lines
the hazards of the bight
he chortles at the chore
and sets perspectives straight

The wit of wounding days
is evident to few —
he knows it in his toes
and cries it to the crew
till raw resentments die
and angry tensions ease
and he has made us see
beyond the mournful trees

They shoe you like a horse
and shove you up a hill
and lead you to believe
your life's a bitter pill
But he's a cheerful sort —
a chaffer at the chaff
The rain beats down like blame
and still he makes me laugh

I lurch in leaky boots
until the claim is raped
I wince in witless winds
until a hurt is shaped
Then suddenly a voice
lampoons my epitaph
and hell, he lets me live
and hell, he makes me laugh.

Joshua

John Joshua and I
just about fought our own private
Battle of Jericho
on the cable-scarred mountains
above Christy Cove

Never had any trouble
with Indians before
but Joshua was another matter —
Red Power radical —
hated white men worse than Monday morning

That ill-natured sonofabitch
got on my case from the first day
as though I were personally to blame
for every outrage
his people were ever subjected to

If Joshua had been white
I wouldn't have suffered his guff for long
but I had some foolish idea
about racial tolerance
so I took the abuse for a week or two

Still, enough of this sort of treatment
would drive even Gandhi to pick up a gun —
the guy was a bastard in any man's language —
I built up a log-jam of anger
and one day he kicked loose the king-stick

We were out alone by the tail-blocks
when my patience blew like a shot stump —
In someone else's voice
I warned John Joshua to get off my back
so driven by fury, I frightened myself

He looked more surprised than outraged —
his trained worm had turned —
we stood toe to toe on the sidehill
but Joshua's money was not where his mouth was —
his eyes slid away   he walked off muttering

Next morning, I learned Joshua had quit —
perhaps it was only coincidence
but word went round camp that I'd run him off
I didn't dispute the rumour —
it tasted sweet like a hot rum in winter

The Trackers

Sixteen miles from camp
locking the day around us
fog fills the gaps between the hemlocks
Two men on a stamped and hammered mountain
we monkeywrench our idle loader
waiting for the logging trucks

White man? Indian? We are simply loggers
watched by the same impartial clouds
riding a battered hill to easy money
waiting for quitting-time   waiting for those trucks
but both our drivers have broken down
for a long time there aren't any

Somewhere, a long way below us
we can hear the faint whistles of the steeltower
our diligent buddies are pulling more country apart
We're up here among the foggy ridge trees
wagon-scouts of the highest timber   getting bored
running out of bullshit   grinding our cigarettes in the dirt

"Hey, look at the deer sign!" says Joe, pointing
We track it along the rain-packed road
stalk it past the great stalks of the trees with the mist billowing
lost to the lockstepping world
And it is more than freshmade hoofprints
more than the nervous proof of wildlife we are following

It is a deeper thing dredged from ancestral memory
flashing from the backchambers of the brain
a sense of forgotten identity   a glimpse of some intrinsic Creature
We are moving in more than the direction of our curiosity
caught by some pure current that tugs from the vortex of the dawn
dissolving the facade   reminding us of our essential nature

But enough of this!   Sounds like a truck coming
Responsibility taps us with a reproving finger
Time to stumble back to reality   pull up our civilized socks
Sixteen miles from camp
locking the day around us
fog fills the gap between the hemlocks.

The Snow Sadness Of January

The deserted camp
turns its face
to the slow thaw-weather rain
and the yellow cats —
the horned trucks lie dormant

Hypnotic stillness grips the log-dump
granted pause
by winter work-stoppage
for this holiday hiatus

Respited too
from the busy wheels of industry
we sit in the cook-shack
drinking beer
at this breathing-space
assessment point
of our lives

Our talk is drunken
extravagant
predictable
answerless
unproductive
as the suspended camp
in the snow sadness of January.

Cinderwind

When the cinderwind's breath
blew my valley black
the sky was a fevered flush
full of singed crows
and the quick green death

Sap-factories exploding
the trees went up like hair
on a torched woman
along the awakened air
the flayed smoke came riding

Among stampeded machines
below we watched
the gallivanting flames
graffitti the helpless hill
with demented designs

And the cinderwind whipped
a frenzy of glow-worms
to the distant echoing stars
in a cackle of abandon
as the day dipped

Till it reined at the gully
that cut like a mortal wound
down the stump-chimneyed slopes,
barred by its dripping abyss
from the outer valley

Foiled in a snort of sparks
it paced the damp edges
licked the unpalatable rocks
hissed like a dying god
to the hard dark

Kicking through eaten ash
of smouldering aftermath
we hunted its stubborn remnants
with spitting canvas snakes
in the sunflash

Cold snow will accrue
to bandage the savaged earth
in medical winter
to hide the dust-clotted scars
where the cinderwind blew

Waterbomber

When the waterbomber wept
six-thousand gallons
of crushing tears
on the threatened timbercrest
where the confident flames
cantered like demonsteeds,
they died in the thump of a salty second
too overwhelmed to whistle

All their hot dreams of combustion
nipped in the bud
by a whaleweight of wet
as the waterbomber
slow enough to fall
followed its bird-dog plane
through each tree-tapping run
and feathered away, spitting a rainbow.

Mexican Standoff
in memory of Terry Munro

On a day hot enough to crack rocks
the fireweed exploded
filling the air with floating spores
like feathers
from a broken pillow

The fat sky spat down heat
on the raw mountain face —
the hungry machine
demanded logs —
we fed it like fools
to earn our beer money
sweating —
swatting flies and fireweed fluff
in the shimmering swelter

It was the sort of day
that frays a man's nerves like string —
under the hammering sun
our usual good humor melted away

Faced with a stump-jammed cedar
you questioned my judgement
on how to roll it free
until I was forced to pull rank —
a minor argument
exacerbated by the temperature —
we slogged on through the hours
like a couple of deaf mutes
too angry to speak

It was damn near quitting time
when we reached that giant fir
back of the tail block
a classic puzzle in logging logistics
To skin it free was going to require
a cooperative effort
I looked at you   you looked at me
we both smiled   the stubborn impasse broke
the hatchet was buried
We set to work
parbuckled the big blue-butt out of there
and became friends again.

Trackloader

Trackloader squats
birdlike on the mountain's edge
mainline dangling
from the beak of its boom
like a steel worm
wrenched from the ruined earth

Yellow gridarm swings
above a half-loaded truck
against the green of the valley wall
mauve flush of fireweed
cloudy turquoise sea
sunfired emerald islands
dim blue city through rainscrubbed distance
gray volcanic peak of another country

Dieselfuming tyrant of my days
in whose control cab, Fullbore Bill
one-gear engineer from the steampot past
tugs and bounces those suffering sticks
across the blasted slopes
bangs a near-miss choker at me
forgetfully unsafe beside a stump

In these hours of joy and jeopardy
I eat a pound of mountain blueberries
while Haywire Denny spells me
We sweat out the weekend beer
laugh like fools at the danger
whoop and holler the day away
head up the hill at last
alive exhausted happy
into the quitting-whistle's echo

The Finishing

    Last day   last hour   last log
        big grizzled fir butt
  lead-heavy with pitch   seesawing
   on the lip of a hundred-foot hole
  There's two or three more good pieces
     down in that spooky pit —
   they can bloody well stay there —
only a chopper could harvest those bastards

    Last day   last hour   last log
   I take my time with it   easing
  ragged cable around rough bark
     in the familiar ritual
I punch the whistle   the choker snaps taut
    the fir butt shakes alive —
   shudders up from its death bed —
    crunches towards the spar-tree

    Last day   last hour   last log
  a sense of relief   a sense of sadness —
  now I will run in the lines and blocks —
  we have had our way with this mountain
     Another woodwar won —
   another forest felled and stolen —
another notch on some timber king's desk —
   another virgin hill ahead of us

Skookumchuck

Reprieved for a merciful moment
from repetitive conversation
in the ramshackle evening bunkhouse,
I watch the alders move like great grey reeds
to a wrinkling wind
below the ruined watersheds   wrung slopes
where new roads snake past the snowline
and the black amputated claws
of charred stumps
grip dirt in the scarcountry

I have stumbled back to the woods
after drunken years of absence
driven again by several needs —
found my way to this woebegone place
of weatherbattered buildings
where a disused landing barge
landed forever
rusts in the bushes
like all my hamstrung dreams

Sing a song of recompense —
noisy joshing suppertimes
in a cookhouse with a broken guthammer

Sing a song of necessity
in this ancient logging camp
by the tidal rapids called Skookumchuck
which means Strong Water
and must be drunk
beyond bottles.

The Animals

The second marten
I've ever seen
eyes us in glittering assessment
before moving rapidly along a dead log
a streamlined package of brown wariness
to become the forest again

Two deer
deploy through the distance
tiptoe nervously
through the first thin snow
watch curiously
as we fumble cold cables

Only the whiskyjacks
display any regret
vying for our lunchtime leavings
with an extra grey urgency
to top off winter caches
in obscure hollow trees

November's feathers
twitch from a colourwrung sky
settling like a white moss of reprieve
on the wrecked hill
Blood oozes from a hemlock stump
as I savage its bark with a chainsaw

We are mackinawed transgressors
in mudcaked boots
cursing and blessing the freighted wind
as the day dwindles
the season takes aim on us
and the animals know

Grease For The Wheels Of Winter

Quickening in the valley, the white flutter
blurs the road-slashed relief-map   The valleyfloor
tips in the salted distance   Such damp confetti
will wed these boondocks to quiet

But yet, the engines grunt   lines tighten and thrash
against the spooked sky   men stamp and laugh
beside hemlock fires   trucks wheeze   remote radio voices
direct woodwar   We are still at our bothersome business

And then we are shrugging from skins of wet raingear
lighting cigarettes   eating apples   lying a mean lick
rattling towards warmth in the quittingtime crummy
past killed machines like abandoned yellow elephants

Behind us, the old house of the land reclaims silence
Soon the snow will cover the broken floors and furniture
with a single sheet
No one will unlock these doors again until spring
Rigging will hang like forgotten laundry from
clotheslinepole spar-trees

Only the wind will come then to croon in the spared boughs
of trees too high or meagre to kill   The white, the white
flutter and smile of silence will spread from ear to ear
and nod this place calm like a mother

The Dead

They're never too far away
the dead I stumble the hills with...

Billy Turgenoff
had his guts torn out
when a guyline stump pulled
in the bad old days,
my brother's brief partner
sold short early
leaning against a bunkhouse
forever nineteen
in the faded photograph

Verne Turner
old ally of kickaround camps
companion of bunkhouse and bar,
got married
and drowned off a Queen Charlotte's boom
in the same year

Finn Billy
the mad sky-hanger
finally played out his luck —
a fresh-topped spar split open on him —
crushed him against his rope —
he died of a busted back

Gary Allenby
logging in avalanche country
was crushed like an insect under a rockslide
in a rainstorm —
became a statistic in the obituary columns
and although I never knew him
I knew him

I envision all
the imaginable calamities
as a breaking mainline
bullwhips the clouds —
as a runaway fir butt
with designs on my hide
batters by me down a dry watercourse

They're never far away
the dead I stumble the hills with
in the risk and the rain
but I will stumble with them
as long as the madness lasts
touch wood
or don't.

The Ridge Trees

Distantly on stone ridges
the highest trees lean wearily
like old men
in Oriental paintings
shuffling eternally before the wind

Helicopter clacks down the valley
chopper preceding the choppers
airborne timber tallier
counting the moneyherds
of the untouched conifers

Next year we will practice havoc
in that green trench —
the saws will yammer their nagging dirge —
the donkeys will gather the corpses —
the land will be hammered to stumps and ruin

And when our depredations are done
only the twisted ridge trees will stand
above the brown carnage
like meditative old men
shuffling eternally before the wind

ically remembered her. Then the lights dimmed. The Remembering was about to begin.

THE REMEMBERING

A Testament Of Hills

It was pulling strawline
up some endofnowhere hill
in the rain
with the whole world tied to the end —
reefing like a lunatic
on a piece of steel string
with no hand free to swat the horseflies

It was Friday afternoons
of drythroats and beerthirst —
wahooing down washouts
with the quittingtime whistle
sounding reprieve —
shave and a haircut
six bits

It was riding those doodlebug planes
up craggy inlets —
bouncing through the airpockets
in gutgrabbing skips and hops
to land with queasy relief —
caulk-boots and a duffel-bag
at some forlornshack camp

It was a block breaking
with a spar-tree half raised —
the tree smashing back into the swamp —
part of the block whistling by your head
like angry shrapnel
and in your mouth the rusty taste of death
for the first time

It was trying to unhook floating logs
with greenhorn fingers
in the churning bull-pen
of an A-frame show —
the hardnosed engineer
busting a gut with laughter
each time you hit the shivering drink

It was sometimes the inviting eyes
of a faller's wife
dangerous with discontent and townhunger —
bored with isolation and her husband's
rough and seldom hands —
enticing reluctant chokerboys
into scaredstiff affairs

It was the cooleyed logger junkies
kicking heroin habits in sullen bunkhouses —
cynical victims of too many
underworld winters —
boasting of successful scores —
getting back in shape for another
tussle with the monkey

It was the wattled faces
of reamedout oldtimers
reduced to bedmaking
and shrill recollection —
watching the crummies and campboats leave
for the steep morning hills
in arthritic envy

And it was deadly dull
bunkshack Sundays
in the windy lonesome wilderness
relieved by the toothless wit
of the camp comic
who knew every dirty joke there was
and a few more

It was working three suicide shows
in a row
too broke or stupid to quit —
logs and boulders crashing down on you
through blinding clammy fog —
an uprooted stump chasing you one day
and nearly catching you

It was the skidroad hiring-halls
with their seedy wheedling mancatchers —
their beckoning job-listing blackboards
and the travel vouchers that committed you
to early-morning airstrips
and another resigned plunge
into the familiar unknown

It was letting the last guyline go
on a stripped spar-tree —
watching it quiver and topple
like a sabotaged tower
to crash back to earth
in a second downfall
for only raised trees died more than once

It was the legendary characters —
Dirty Dick —
Boomstick Annie —
Eight-and-Biscuits Bronson —
Johnny on the Spot —
some actually met in careless camps —
most remaining myths

It was walking to the wharf
on listless Jervis Inlet evenings
full of impatient energy
even the sidehills couldn't sap —
yearning for the bright lights
and that elusive something beyond them
you couldn't quite name

And it was unreal early shifts
in the tinder days of fire-season
standing on dim slopes
as light crawled over the farthest ridge —
beating off the insects
who ruled the summer dawns —
hearing the starting whistle blow

It was fighting fire —
wearing back-packs and eating smoke —
tugging hoses through a no-man's land
of sparks and charcoal —
sitting all-night fire-watch
with the mountain smouldering around you
like a medieval hell-vision

It was evil days of high wind and hail
with saplings snapping like straws
and your hands numb
and your mind numb
and your feet soaking wet
and a log-hungry company-loving hooker
too chintzy to shut her down and go home

It was the ubiquitous cookshack
centre of every camp's humdrum universe
where the grub was sometimes good
sometimes bad   but always plentiful
and once you saw a cook take after a man
with a meat-cleaver
just like in Bob Swanson's poem

It was the beer-parlor bull-sessions
where the toughest shows were yarded —
the highest log-counts taken —
the tallest trees topped —
the closest shaves experienced
and every whistle-punk
was hooktender for a night

It was three glum months
on an obscure stinking tideflat
somewhere northeast of nowhere
where the rain was constant
wolves prowled at night
and once the boatman got drunk with the supplies
and you went on short rations for a week

And it was the last camp —
the deadliest show of them all —
ground so treacherous
the hooktender whistled in disbelief
You stuck it out for awhile
but the fear got you in the end
so you quit the logging camps forever —
until the next time.

Hoodoo Cove

Gaunt buildings beckon
beyond a dripping wall of alders
draw me up a tangled trail
to stand before a doorless bunkhouse
so enormous
the farther end of its corridor
is only a tiny rectangle
of rain-polished light

I move towards it and enter
boots tapping ghosts awake
in the mildewed rooms
with their rusty iron bedsteads —
empty window sockets —
breached ceilings weeping water

A decomposing dartboard
hangs limp and pitted
on a central wall
Dimly I hear lost laughter —
the careful thuds of evening contests —
but the loggers are thirty years gone

Four hundred men
worked this outfit once
until a plague of teredoes
drilled the booms to trash
After only three years
the site was abandoned

Back at the beach, the log-dump
its planks pulpy with age —
its donkey engine
corroding on a moss-furred platform
like a forgotten idol
points shakily across the bay
where an Indian hand-logger
last inhabitant of this unlucky place
moves distantly
like a prophecy
against the sinister green trees.

A Man Gone Mad With Logging

A man gone mad with logging
has cut his roommate's throat for no cause
stolen a boat this cold camp Sunday
rows the bay in eccentric circles
Making no further move to escape.
he lets out a howl every so often
like a maimed animal in a trap
The world is his waking nightmare now

We have worked with this man run amok
wrestled logs with him in the rain
shared noon coffee   tall yarns
the shocks   knocks and jokes of the trade
On the hunched mountain shoulders
we have seen him hurl his hat in a rage —
heard him call God's bluff in a cloud —
but this is the normal madness of loggers

Had he cast off his mind in the hills
he might well have seized up an axe —
vented that pent-up fury on us —
such things have been known to happen
Once in an up-Island camp
a clumsy third-loader, mocked by the crew
smuggled a rifle to work —
fed his tormentors bullets for lunch

But Silver O'Grady religiously
saved up his madness for Sunday
He watched camp last winter   was too long alone
Now the dam of his wits has broken
He rows in ragged erratic circles
A seaplane banks in over the inlet
A man has gone mad with logging
The coppers are coming to take him away.

Ghostcamp

A lot of loggers hide dead in these hills
setting chokers eternally
on healed slopes above brush-choked landings
where rusting steampots
crouch sphinxlike and voiceless
and corroded snake cables
twist paralyzed among the ferns
with motion, a steel memory

In the empty camp that lies
half-ransacked at the northern mouth
of this ransacked valley,
we stand thoughtful among ruin —
ancient bull-blocks
sleep like giant turtles in the weeds —
heavy two-man power-saws
lie forever unmended in sheds

Garages full of obsolete bearings —
abandoned anvils —
blacksmiths and mechanics gone
to whatever random destiny
The gutted bunkhouse guards echoes
fled dreams of drifted men
with few dreams   the cookshack
guthammer hasn't clanged for years

I have come full circle   Across
the inlet lies Misery Creek
where my brother and I watched camp
one fireseason summer two decades back
The dead camp sprawls around us
I can't speak   it's too strange
Log long enough, you're bound to stumble
across your own bootprints in the end.

Logger's Rain

The kind of soft autumn rain
it was good to work in the woods in
tickles from a tarnished sky
the roof of my idle cover
trickles from the hard-hat rims
of all my peers and successors
who slog the stumpslopes yet
on the mountains I've fled forever

Almost two years since I lost
my last caulk-boots on purpose
my torn rainclothes too
and the gloves just one day worn
slung them under the crummy seat
for next year's greenhorns to find
laughed through the shutdown snow
free as a sprung con

Destiny's punk in a dream
aboard that lasttime boat
I blew strange smoke in the backseats
with the newway forest kids
watched by amused old fallers
bound for the Hastings' hotels
the familiar skidroad sabbaticals
in their hoarded holiday duds

Quit three times but this one's for real
I'll never go back   not ever
except in my mind to the chokers
the hillsweat   the game you can't win
But it's two years later   The rain falls
down the homesick sky like a memory
the kind of soft autumn rain
it was good to work in the woods in

Ghosts Have No Money To Spend

      Country of clawed islands
jigsaw puzzle of channels and passageways
     where clouds melt into snow
along coast mountains shouldering aside
       pale sky in sunstrewn april

       Boat plods doggedly
through waters white with small waves
    orange with migrant kelp
      to Minstrel Island
      prickly with memories

      Time-blurred faces
    half-forgotten voices
   distant roistering dreams
   of celebrant Saturdays
in this rough-hewn place with the musical name

  Save for us, the bar sits empty
logger-scarred   much smaller than recalled
    How in hell did they all fit
in the heyday years when the gyppo camps
  strung their A-frames around this hub
    like a single letter alphabet?

"They was stacked in here like cordwood"
says Pearlie behind the bar, remembering
  "Old Abie ran it then   He used to say:
    'Gentlemen, we are now closed'
  when the boys got to tanglin' asses
  and 'Gentlemen, we are now open'
    when they was finished"

His voice has a wistful edge
for the boom years are gone forever
The floor of Minstrel's bay is cobbled with bottles
but ghosts have no money to spend.

Elephant's Graveyard

      Two A-frames
      bob side by side
  in rickety obsolescence —
        the oldest
hasn't yarded a log for years
its rust-chewed donkey-engine crouches
    like an impotent sphinx
   below the spraddle-legged
moss-patched triangle of the sticks

As though the glory-day Fifties
have come to this quiet cove to die,
the floatcamp slumps down in the water
    like an old animal accepting
  the blunt fact of its transience —
     time is running out
on these stubborn gyppo loggers —
     all their days and ways

They are some of the last holdouts
   in this evacuated country —
  tonight, with wry resignation,
    they speak of leaving too
as we drink beer and rum together
in the elephant's graveyard of a bay
       with this day —
    all the days and ways
dying inexorably around us.

The Faller's Story
for Bill Dockar

Tailgunner in the big ones
riding scared to war in a flimsy shell
flak may crack like an egg
or black-crossed hunters come stuttering lead
through the searchlights and shrapnel
unstopped by your bucking barrage
knocking you out of the clouds

Tireless Lancasters
plodding through ack-ack chatter
each slim-odds mission
and you with them   hunched
at your sitting-duck post

A specimen in a plexiglass bubble
you play the russian roulette of battle
across booby-trapped skies
pitching your payloads down
till fire-stormed citadels burn like pitch
and your war bird dodges for home
though unlucky sisterships puke chutes and die

Somehow your number never comes up
Always you gain the Channel
Often crippled   an engine gone
you thump down safe on the tarmac
with something dying back down inside you
no wet-mess whiskey can ever replace

"And that's why I went falling trees," you said
"The adrenaline rush as much as the money
Too many missions gives you the taste for it
Guess there was lots of them came out like me."

Chainsaws In The Cathedral
for Al Purdy

    Morning the crumpled land the hills
        heaving up the sky the rain
    beating down like blood the darkness
    lifting from the trees the waste place
        where trees were leaving
        a gray residue of mist

    Camp at the mountain's foot men
grunting from bunks hawking grumbling back
      into splinterwalled sockstink
    of bunkhouse reality struggling
    into dirtstiff overalls straggling
breakfastwards to the guthammer's jangle

Soon the crummies will strain up the switchbacks
    with men for the mountain the song
  will be sung again in the high hard places
      donkeys will roar on the ridges
     chainsaws whine in the cathedral
of virgin trees, the harsh mad music of loggers.

The Old Campaign

Dynamite
makes the earth vomit boulders
in the high stony hills
where the lastditch trees remain
The harsh song of gunpowder
rattles down the ridges —
they are blasting fresh roads
to ruin in the rain

This valley
has been under siege before —
a task force of steam donkeys
had their way and went
High stumps and alderpaths
speak mutely of their passing
in the twicegrown forest
where the old scars slant

Now below, among them
avenues of new invasion
crosshatch and finger
their raw rutted tracks
Along them we advance
like a raggletaggle army
in toysoldier hardhats
and sulphuryellow trucks

This valley
chokes down a workday dose of us
each battleweary morning
for the faceless men at desks —
suffers our indignities —
our belligerent transgressions —
coughs us up gladly
in the quittingwhistle dusk

The new timber's
bowlingpin battalions
fall to angry chainsaws
in the old campaign
The harsh song of gunpowder
rattles down the ridges —
they are blasting fresh roads
to ruin in the rain.

The Mountains; The Valley

    Constant as clockwork
    the loaded logging trucks
      rumble down the gut
       of the hot valley —
  shout their radio warnings
       along the river

  We dodge one after another
Janosch, our guide, expatriate alpinist
who knows the Matterhorn   the Eiger,
lauds the mountains we move among —
     has scaled their walls —
       skied their slopes

They own the valley, those peaks —
   waterfalls whiten their cliffs
as the snows weep under summer
  The road narrows   forks
     Above low trees
  the strange pinnacle rises

it's a rotting tooth of decaying rock
  Janosch admits he doesn't care
   or dare to tackle that one
    it's a crumbling witchtower
     eroding into rubble
   among the healthier hills

        The road snakes right again
         through logged-off vistas
   green with fireweed and reseeded fir —
    not battleground-ugly in distance
    but like miles of alpine meadow
tipping up to scrub and more white summits

          Around us now
      the househuge boulders
     of an ancient rockslide
that built its town of ruin before men came
     Beyond, a glory hole of stumps
      pitching to the glacial river
    Far ahead, a black monolith
    moults snow in remote ranges
  it's a volcanic plug, Janosch tells me,
    jammed like a gigantic cork
    in the mouth of a dead crater
    He has trodden its lava-top too

  High to our right, a shale-sided Sphinx
       broods against blue
  Below it, a pencil-small steel-spar
       fishes far slopes —
whistles float down   lines twitch silver —
kicking across the hill, the catch comes in

Homebound down the valley,
Janosch, whose task is to heal and restore —
who is the mountain-walker and valley-mender,
tells me of the beekeeper
who plants his hives in the fireweed forests
stealing simple honey from these hills.

The Poem Rower
for Curt Lang

No day for much
this glum grumbler
sky full of dirty cloud —
a spasmodic wind
tangling in the antenna
making the images twitch

Better to sit indoors
by the seaward window
watching the lone beachcomber
stubborn as the buffeted birds
salvaging runaway logs
with a rowboat

They say he writes poems sometimes —
perhaps he is writing one now
of oarlock-creak
wave-slap
and the grunts of his dogged progress
to the last line of the tie-up float.

The Dream Shift

Two seaplanes pull their sounds
across the Sound
above this logrobber's land
against a pale sky
to somewhere north of my inertia
perhaps a wave-slapped dock
where half a crew's quit for the hell of it
and waits with caulkboots tied to their baghandles

Two seaplanes pull my mind
through cobweb walls
to where I left my last bad woodsdream
wetly quivering —
all the worst sidehills of my life
become one impossible panorama —
a thousand riggingmen anting across it —
a hundred haywire donkeys thundering above them

Everything but the kitchen sink
is charging downmountain on those poor bastards —
it's hell's own bowling alley
with a lot of dancing damnfools for pins
I'm both above and among them
both dodger and watcher
caught in the bight of my fantasies —
feeling the rush of remembered adrenaline

Behind the lines like an armchair general
I hear the distant battlecrash
and run the hills I rebuild in the night
in camps I can never quit.

A Crooked Coliseum For The Wind

The vanquished valley
swims in and out of mist
in the morning when the machines
make their warm-up clanks and snorts —
chatter with anticipation
in the tentative rain

The vanquished valley
is a crooked coliseum for the wind
with no trees for it to sing through —
a rough bowl ribbed
with roads that lead nowhere
across slopes of well-considered devastation

The vanquished valley
shrugs unconcernedly
as the sun spills emeralds along the ridges
It will reclothe itself in unfathomable time
when we are gone beyond reckoning
with our insect energies and sweats.

The Slidingback Hills

The hills are sliding back
slipping into a distance
more profound than mere miles
floating into remoteness
down time's wrong-way telescope

The hills are blurring bluely
into a land of spent winds   lost rains
sunken suns   shrunken snows
broken trees   broken friends
sounds of chaos shivering into silence

Dark birds spin like wind-flung leaves
across an ice-pale sky
cold smoke of mist coils between the columns
of vanished virgin forests
phantom rigging crews
toil across torn slopes
and someone I once was
toils dimly with them
a prisoner of memory marooned
in a shadowy caulk-boot kingdom
trapped forever
among the slidingback hills.

The Last Spar-Tree On Elphinstone Mountain
for Al Purdy

The last spar-tree on Elphinstone mountain
through drunken sunday binoculars
pricks the blue bubble of the sky
on that final ridge where the scar tissue peters out
Been four years quiet now on the battered mountain's back
except for shakecutters   hunters   and stray philosophers
The trucks are elsewhere   some of the drivers dead
and the donkeys gone to barber another hill

I'm always shooting my mouth off about mountains
sometimes climbing them
and sometimes just distantly studying them like this
My eyes need no caulk boots
I can vault to that ridge in my mind
stand at the foot of that tree, forlorn as a badly-used woman
become merely landmark and raven perch
I can touch its bark sun-warm as flesh
feel the engines still shaking it functional
with vibrations that never quite die

It's either a cornfield or a catastrophe
Either a crop or a tithe or a privacy
has been taken from this place
What matter?   it's done   Beyond that ridge is a valley
I helped hack and alter   There's a gully there
three-hundred feet deep in places
where we tail-holted on its rim
Dizzy abyss that scared the wits out of me
you furrow down the mountain like God's own drainage ditch
and stopped a forest fire in 1965

At your foot is the dirtiest show of them all
where we logged in the box canyon with debris crashing down
and the rotten hemlock snags trembled over
and the haulback stumps pulled out like bad teeth
and the hooktender said: "She's a natural-born bitch"
and the lines broke and the omens spoke
and I quit from fear to become a brief boomman

I'm getting melodramatic again but it's hard not to
Logging's larger than life   Keep your sailors and cowboys
And I'm always stressing the sombre side
there was much of comradeship and laughter
great yarns beside noon donkeys   hillhumour between turns
excellent shits behind stumps with the wind fanning the stink away
even sweat smelling good and cigarette smoke, celestial

Dream on in peace, old tree
perhaps you're a truer monument to man
than any rock-top crucifix in Rio De Janeiro

A Mountain Shudders Through Me

A mountain shudders through me time and over
the roads that twist its ridges scar my shoulders
the severed logs swim errant down my bloodstream
the hoarse machines are growling in my tissues
Too bleak   too hard   too broken are the highgrounds
I see again those precincts of our plunder
and count within me like an incantation
three joys of wood   three woes of wood   a portent

My world rotates around a ragged axis
of nervous six-gun whistles banged like bullets
to make the cabled rigging dance or tumble
my dangerous steel playmate of the sidehill
My world careens around a splintered vortex
of rainfat cedars strangled to the landing
of uphill, uphill in the sullen morning
of downhill, downhill when the day has freed us

I am a ghost who walks the shattered acres
I am a wraith who haunts the ravaged places
a pawn of weather's stinging pins and needles
of judas fogs and come-a-cropper snowslopes
of boozy sweat that rivers down the forehead
when monday sun is taxing celebration
of jagger wounds and bruises in the bugclouds
Ah God, but it's a madman's occupation!

And once I saw a stump move in the slashwaste
become a bear and patch the distance blackly
an audience of one who watched us coldly
his great cocked head, a blot of disapproval
He'd seen us come and go, that burly beggar
whitefaced intruders born to savage beauty
Soon we'd be gone again   He shrugged his shoulders,
showed us his rump and prowled away disdainful

Above the clouds I lurch, a lowly clumper
with harebrained dreams and a destructive manner
I could as well be stoking up volcanoes
or teaching spinning lessons to a spider
But still the hill's my pleasure and my anger
The thawfloods stroke my eyes and feed my wonder
like quick white horses laughing in a graveyard
A mountain shudders through me time and over

The Alders

The alders are the reoccupiers
they come easily and quick
into skinned land
rising like an ambush
on raked ridges
jabbing like whiskers
up through the washedout
faces of neverused roads

The alders are the forestfixers
bandaging brown wounds
with applegreen sashes
filling in for the fallen firs
jostling up by the stumps
of grandfather cedars
leaning slim to the wind
by logjammed
loggerleft streams

The alders are the encroachers
seizing ground the greater trees owned
once
but no more

It is the time of the alders
they come
like a bright upstart army
crowding
the deadwood spaces
reaching
at last for the hand of the whole
unshadowed sun

The Legends

The King Of Rhymes And Whistles
for Robert Swanson

Doggerel hero, spurred on by Bob Service,
your ballads banged through my boyhood —
Rough House Pete Olesen rampaged through my mind —
the Big Swede Logger gallumphed through my dreams
The Woods you described were a storybook place —
a northern Old West with loggers for cowboys —
a larger-than-life world of caulk-booted tough guys
storming the hills like Paul Bunyan's children

Time had its way and I came to the jungles —
laced my first caulks on and stumbled to battle —
found that your woods kingdom had a few drawbacks —
bugs, hellish weather and wall-to-wall danger
I stuck with the racket, too foolish to quit —
shrugged off the punches and found my own poems
but the loggers had yours by heart, Bob Swanson —
you were their king of rhymes and whistles

Many years after, we sat on a stage
telling our poems and stories together —
you, the old trouper   me, the rank upstart
stirring the memories   stoking the legends
Now you've hired out to those Holy Ghost camps
with a rucksack of myths   a suitcase of echoes
leaving a boy in an aging man's body
still hearing your whistles and heeding your rhymes.

Bullpuncher
for George McGinnis

In the old man's spiderscrawl you read:
"My grandaddy was a teamster —
worked the woods for Jerry Rogers
back round eighteen sixty two" —
somethings tugs from a long distance
new trees slide back into the ground —
old trees rise like lost sentries
and you are more him than you
In the rumbling belly of the past
tasting whiskey   wanting more — and women —
stamping through Gassy Jack's on Saturday
with last week's wages in your hand —
sure like to bed that pretty young one
but you ain't handsome and you smell bad —
fat Bessie with the bad teeth
is all you're ever bound to find —
The madam with her hand out   whorehouse piano
tinkling bright brassy ditties —
brief tumbles on soiled backroom sheets —
then it's time for you to go
back to the bullteams and the hollering —
checking harnesses and chainhooks —
bound to get a few more week's hauling
before the deep snow —
bound to shout 'em uptrail   downtrail
till the light won't allow it —
sends you trudging down the skidroad home
for more bacon and navy beans —
maybe fresh biscuits if you're lucky
and that bellyrobber didn't burn 'em —
certainly coffee, strong as gall

and later on, the old complaints
that men have always made in bunkhouses —
in army barracks   in mine cages —
in ship's holds   assuredly in gaol
when the warders couldn't hear
till the lamps are snuffed at nine thirty —
you drop like a pig into a pit —
leave your aching muscles behind you —
seek the solace of the unaware
drink deep the medicines of the dark
beyond oxen, sullen whores and hangovers —
beyond the griping and the belching —
the bloody cooties and the damp —
too spent to dream more than simply
of anything except oxen, trees and rain —
drown in oblivion like a sea
till it's daylight in the swamp —
rise stiffly in the unforgiving dawn —
the bulls wait patient for your goadstick —
someone curses groggily   your socks stink —
outside it's still raining —
it's a hell of a way to make a dollar
but you'll do it long as your legs last —
the guthammer writes strident on the air
the cold truths of morning.

The Country Of The Bull
for Gordon Gibson Sr.

Beyond the blacktop's end
the road runs wild
through raw and ravaged land
from duncecap peaks
rambunctious rivers crash
beneath log bridges
the rough way twists and climbs
tips, dips and sheers
The gravel slides like ice
beneath the wheels
blind corners loom
we fear for logging trucks
The last hills wave us past
we crest the summit of a final ridge
through parting trees, the ancient inlet blinks
and we are in the Country of the Bull

This limberlost
remote   aloof   exhilarating land
was once his bailiwick
Across these slopes
along these waterways when youth ran strong
he beat his measured path
the gawky boy became the looming man
he squared off with the trees
spat on his hands and taught himself to log

Bull of the Woods
they called him for his stormblast of a voice
and his ox-stubborn ways   unquenchable
his thirst for timber (and the other stuff)
he slaked it to the full
In his spare time, he fished and flew a plane
ran sawmills, captained ships and carved his mark
then by a wild river, he sat down
and breached a crock of scotch
and dreamed a town

The Bull has long forged on
to other schemes in places far removed
The town he dreamed remains
around the sawmill at the valley's mouth
those first rude shacks
have burgeoned into modern houses now
a bullish legacy
a thriving outport at the inlet's head
a monument to that unflinching man
who thundered it from nothing long ago

Grandaddy Tough
for Gordy Dewar

Grandaddy Tough's
got a history of logging
in his hard hands
the cold-decked memories
lie eager for the telling

he's old and young
the manfires
smoulder yet in him
He has stripped more sidehills
than I'll ever know
lost spar trees
shudder in his eyes

He has walked with legends
and all unknowing
become one
beyond the heyday of his boots
the forests thrown down
regrown
and thrown down again

He roars yet
in the power of his age
a leather veteran
of the mountain wars
splendid in drink
a thousand bar chairs behind him
since the first lifted whisky
the first fat stake
pissed grinning down the drain

In the sweaty dusk
of forgotten bunkhouses
he has gambled with long-dead rigging rats
and tumbled to his bunk
to sleep the timber sleep

Among boys he walks
careless with experience
Grandaddy Tough
a bridge of gristle
between then and now

The steampots   the skylines
rust on remembered ridges
but he lurches on
under trees of steel
in the knotty triumph of his trade

Logger Hunt

That morning they are standing there   the whole
impatient lot of them   unkindly clustered
on our camp dock   deliberately clutching
their phallic guns in itchy hands   unloading
trail bikes from their fancy rich man's yacht
with the pearl portholes   "Hey now, where the hell
you think you're going?" shouts Duluth, the super,
his face gone white with outrage   "This here land
is private goddamn property!"   He stops
seeing the guys mean business   "You loggers
are going to make our day" declares a crewcut
ex-army type with cold astringent eyes
"We're here to hunt   Head for the bush, you bastards!
You're the prey!"

At first we think it's all some crazy joke
but something in their manner tells us different
We back off from the guns   then turn and run
towards the shelter of the trees   spurred on
by random shots wasp-whining by   What nightmare
has conjured us from loggers into quarry
mere game for maniacs   two-legged deer
condemned to homicidal hide-and-seek?
Ten minutes start they've given us   we scatter
like desperate convicts bolting from the bloodhounds
alive with common fear

The scrubby forest swallows us   I tumble
unthinking over windfalls   gash my knee
and feel nothing but the icy fist
of panic where my heart was   it is time
to learn the craft of foxes   gasping on
I strike a deer-path   run its winding course
reach the spring-angry river   find a tree
that forms a bridge   essay its shaky length
a rat upon a rope above the torrent
attain the farther shore and scrabble up
a brushy slope until I gain a rock bluff
fall flat upon its brow

Here, panting, hidden, safe — perhaps — I watch
the green invaded valley   gunfire rattles
across the river, strident in the morning —
death prowls those woods now angry as a cancer —
among the trees the hunters move to murder
And, as I watch, a man breaks to the creekside —
it's old Duluth, the super, spent and wheezing —
he's hit   I see the crimson welling blood
He totters there unsurely   gives a groan
and tumbles in the flood

His executioner comes into view
and gazes round him with a puzzled air
a slab-faced man, his rifle cocked and ready
to finish off the job but dead Duluth
is riding to the sea   The hunter spits
sits on a rock and fires a fat cigar
then terrifyingly, he lifts his head
and stares directly at my hiding place
I worm down in the moss
certain he must have spotted me   preparing
to flee again but finally he grunts
stabs out the stogie   stalks away to find
another man to hunt

All deadly day the deadly sport goes on
the rifles rattle   once I hear a cry
but no one tracks me to my rocky lookout
the sun's a bloody echo in the sky
and I can only hide in silent horror
as one by one, my harried comrades die

At last the rifles cease   the sated hunters
tramp back to camp   the gory rout is over
I see the yacht cast loose
and cruise off innocently down the inlet
I must recross the river
knowing that I may be the sole survivor
of this mad game   vowing that nevermore
will I hire out for any wage or reason
to work the woods when loggers are in season.

Truckjammer
In memory of Steve Littlejohn

On a murderous mountain road
you lost the air to your brakes
and started your desperate skid —
three hundred feet you plunged
down that eighty-eight percent hill
but they couldn't kill you, kid

Flung clear a hundred feet down
in the path of runaway logs
who'd have laid odds you'd live?
But somehow that avalanche
passed you and thundered by —
chose to let you survive

They couldn't believe your luck
when they flew you broken and bruised
back from that closeshave claim
but I had cause to believe —
I'd seen you cheat death before
more than one risky time

I'd known you far too long
since we were both hometown boys
and knocked back the whiskey plain
in those first gunnybag camps
where we sold our sweat to the hills
for the sake of other men's gain

I'd known you far too long
when you packed a pistol for kicks
through the hustling racetrack years
but even in hoodlum dreams
beyond the whinny of nags
you heard the whinny of gears

A jockey of trucks, you learned
to jam them down breakneck grades
where the sensible drivers quit —
hit the throttle and go
with a sky-high bunkload of wood
riding your back like a bet

Once by a crumbling cliff
you hung bunkbound on a bend
but you wouldn't desert the load —
held her there on the brink
till we hooked a line to the frame
and hauled you back on the road

You have always shot dice with death —
you will gamble with death again
on those hills of hazard and doubt
with your good eye watching the road
and your glass eye winking at fear
till your nine lives run out.

Tombstone On Goatfoot Mountain

The waiting hill tipped ragged against the sky
in the press of the swelling sun   We shuffled our feet
and talked of oldtime logging in years gone by
on a windless morning of heat

"Back then" said the ancient hooker, shifting his snoose,
"she was rough and tough   They played it by hit or miss
And I've damn sure seen my share of shit and abuse
but never a show like this!

it's kinda funny but when I was young and quick
and my legs were good, they mostly logged on the flat
But now I'm gettin' old" — and he rubbed his neck —
"we gotta work ground like that!"

His eyes and ours gazed up past the steel-spar
that gleaming symbol of modern efficiency
We saw the claim with its rock bluffs rugged and sheer
and we tasted the irony

Then it was starting time   Resigned to our lot
we snuffed our smokes and began the morning ascent
as though we had sinned by living — God, it was hot! —
and this was our punishment

We were damp with sweat when we reached the first of the logs
We took time out for a short but grateful break
and hunkered down on the hillside panting like dogs
while the hooker puffed in our wake

The whistle bansheed   Distant the rigging jerked
into metal motion   Chokers rattled and danced
up-mountain toward us   Hoarsely a raven croaked
And so the yarding commenced

We throttled logs with our prickly steel ropes —
logs that had stood as trees before we were born —
Sent them shuddering truckwards down the slope
turn after headlong turn

The day dragged on   The air was a scorching sheath
The only moisture, sweat that daggered the eyes
The snarling sun above   The fools beneath
condemned to scrabble for trees

The cables scraped a tune on the naked rocks
We dreamed of beer in the air-cooled bars of town
and of sparks that might sow flame by the haulback blocks
Much hotter they'd close us down

In our groggy minds we nursed a need for reprieve
It would never come so what the hell was the use?
Then the hooktender yelled   The sidehill came alive
as the roadline stump tore loose

We dived for cover and held by horror, we stared
at the grizzled hooker whose legs were not fast enough
for the spinning uprooted stump that came like it cared
and swept him over a bluff

There's little more   We packed the hooktender out
dead as though he had never breathed or been
and they closed her down but we heard his words like a shout—
"it's the toughest show I've seen!"

His grave lies elsewhere, carefully kept and unmarred
with a floral wreath and a plaque that bears his name
but his real stone is a cliff-face, pitted and scarred
on a logged-off logging claim

Goosequill Snags

Barney Cotter
bought it up in Ramsay Arm
Read it in the papers
twelve years back
Wild log rolling-pinned on him
crushed him against a rock

Barney and I worked together
in Halsam's camp on Goatfoot Mountain
with his chattering chuckle
that broke to a graveyard cough
hurting his way ahead of me up the slopes
burned out from booze and board feet at forty five

Barney was philosophical
"That's the name of the game" he'd say
squinting out from under his hard hat
firing another cigarette
"Always wanted to run a store or something
But I ended up a goddamn logger!"

There were a lot of dead trees on that claim
hollow fire-gutted cedar shells
spiking up among the felled timber
"Goosequill snags" Barney called them
I never forgot the term
It was his only poetry

Barney is long buried
but his goosequill snags still stand
on the mending slopes of Goatfoot Mountain
Lonely monuments
to another man the hills took
writing his rough legend on the sky.

The Last Handfallers
for Bus Griffiths

They're coming up the trail
big blue-veined hands
cramped from a lifetime
of tyrannical wooden handles
of gnawing the big ones down
the hard way
of hearing the undercut timber cry
as it grudgingly gives

They have stoical Svenska faces
white-stubbled
cured to creased red leather
by a many-weathered craft

They have crinkled Svenska voices
like wind in the branches
of the countless killed trees
who have given them their tongues

They are older than rumours
unbending as mountain granite
They have been lured from boozy retirement
to fall the West Fork setting

With their tedious cross-cuts
they will topple the rock-slide cedars
spitting snoose
striving to lessen the breakage

They have returned to the resinous hills
    like ancestral gunslingers
      for one final showdown
     with the reluctant trees

Collision Course

It is a tree of average girth
neither the tallest nor the smallest
it has rolled with the punches
of a hundred mountain storms
and weathered every one

He is the sort of fastidious faller
who mixes his gas with a measuring-cup —
his boots are carefully greased —
they crunch through the remnant snow —
he carries the powersaw casually like a suitcase

The tree shudders
as the chain rips through its growth rings —
the man guides his tool impassively
thinking about his wife and kids —
chips spray like shrapnel —
the engine growls like a wounded cougar —
fibres part before blurring teeth —
the tree quakes   begins to inch
unwillingly from the vertical

The man withdraws the saw   snaps it silent
leans against a stump   gropes for a smoke —
on a tearing hinge of wood
the tree tips   hisses down
but the faller's aim has been faulty
the hemlock strikes a standing cedar
the butt breaks free   kicks back
like a triggered piston

There is no time to run
the butt connects like a wooden hoof
pins the man to the stump
his ribs snap like sticks —
fastidious to the end
he pulls free his wallet
places it safely above the blood
on the tree that has felled him.

Running Scared With The Sky-Hanger
for Bill Macheri

        Finn Billy, you old sky-hanger
      rigging a tree once, so thumping drunk
        you didn't remember doing it —
         monkeying that stick by sheer
            subliminal savvy —
         roping, spiking stubbornly up
to stand at the top like a blasphemous muezzin
      knocking free bark with a blunt axe
        blistering the sky with curses
          calling God to account

        Finn Billy, you sidehill spider
the Compensation Board would have screamed
           in outrage to watch
the day you rode the bull-block up the spar
         for the mad sake of speed
       and later as we gulped to see it
      unfastening your climbing rope —
     tightrope-walking along the skyline
a hundred and twenty feet above the stumps
          to oil the carriage

No, it was not the the giddy hazards you feared
     but something much more nebulous —
   an obscure nemesis chewing like rust
      at the guywires of your sanity

   Once in a back room at a weekend party
     you showed me your private arsenal —
  twenty-five loaded guns in a secret trunk —
        even a Smith and Wesson

"No vun screws with me, kid!"
you muttered unsurely
the sweating terror like an enemy in your eyes
knowing the brain's blackest hounds
need only one
careful bullet.

Horsefly Harry

Insects was never too popular in the woods
Noseeums   Horseflies   Skeeters
Blackflies   Deerflies   Wasps —
sonsofbitches was everywhere —
bite right through leather
some of the mean little bastards

Mostly we just took our lumps
Wasn't a hell of a lot you could do
except pull the pin
and for all a guy knew
he might end up in some gaddam swamp gyppo
where the flies was even worse

We just cussed 'em, killed 'em and kept on logging
But they bothered some guys more than others
Like old Horsefly Harry
He hated horseflies so bad you wouldn't believe it
Liked to catch them alive
"Gotcha, you miserable fucker!" he'd shout

Then he'd take a sliver of toothpick
shove it up the fly's arse
and set it free again
And I swear to God those little sonsofwhores
would shoot straight up into the sky
till you couldn't even see them no more

"Screws up their equilibrium" said Harry
who used to read a lot
Well, I don't know much about that
but they sure as hell did take off
right into orbit for all we knew
just like them gaddam Ruskie Sputniks

Harry, he'd laugh like hell to see them go
Goofy old sonofabitch
he sure did hate horseflies!

Old Hooker Bill

Monday, bloody Monday   the wind's cutting cold
the rain won't let up
and we're stuck here on a sidehill damn near sheer
like a bunch of sitting ducks

Finn Billy is our boss   he's a good-enough old cuss
but he tends to get unhinged
Anytime things go awry, he throws curses at the sky
that'd make a whore cringe

Right now he's spitting mad   howling anger at the snag
where the turn's caught tight
it's the tenth time today   maybe you could say
that he don't live right

But it's his job for sure   a hooktender's chore —
we can relax now —
stamp our feet to keep warm, underneath the drooping arms
of the dripping cedar boughs—

Coax alive wet smokes   swap a few dirty jokes
while the chill wind whinnies
and old hooker Bill goes storming down the hill
to earn his hard money.

The Song
for Stewart W. Holbrook

The song began as a noise in the woods
in wintry Maine when the first ones came
with saws and axes and pungent oath
bound to drag logs to freezing streams —
with stabbing peaveys and monkey legs
ride the freshets and break the jams —
chase the drives to downriver mills
and splinter the boards in the Bangor bars

The song was the moan of a dying kid
crushed by a tree in the life-cheap days
of stinking pallets and snoose-stained floors —
beans and fatback and deacon seats
Traded for greed in the grinding time
of backsore labour from light to dark —
lonely womanless winter nights —
bugs and blisters and damn poor pay

And it was the grunts of bearded men
stamping home in the pinewood dusk —
building the bones of a bunkhouse myth
from blood and gumption and liquor sweat
spinning the yarns on frostblack nights
of a man called Paul and his Big Blue Ox,
mightiest woodsboss of them all
who shook the hills with his earthquake shoes

The song rang on as the crews cut west —
reached the rim of the naked lands —
a daunting sight for a timber beast —
but they braved the plains with the wagon trains —
scaled the continental spine
to gaze on a land of godly trees
clustered thick as hairs on a hound —
mammoth-butted   taller than lies

Now was the song to swell and flood —
the methods altered to meet the needs —
bull-teams bellowed and flumes were built
to chute the timber down to the sea
Soon came spar-trees and roaring shays —
high-speed donkeys powered by steam —
A-frames, chokers and diesel rigs —
cables, chain-saws and wide-bunk trucks

But ever and on, the song was men —
quick-eyed men of a reckless bent
climbing the king-sticks into the sky —
laying them low on the fog-lost slopes —
pulling the levers   setting the beads —
trucking the loads down rip-rap roads —
building the colddecks   swinging them out —
booming the logs at the inlet heads

And ever and on, the song was men —
months-dry men on their skidroad sprees —
blowing their stakes in the waiting towns
on rot-gut whiskey and hungry whores —
flung into drunk-tanks crazed with hooch —
staggering broke to the hiring halls
to strain again on the treadmill hills
with booze-bent faces and small remorse

And ever and on, the song was men —
unschooled men with their secret words —
molly-hogan and whistle-punk —
jill-poke, blue-butt and loading-pot
Ornery men in stagged-off pants —
dirty longjohns and lethal socks —
frayed suspenders and canvas coats —
battered hard-hats and spikey boots

But time has passed and the old song fades —
the Old West faded   the Old Woods fade
The grapple-yarders and steel-spars
replace the rigors of bullwork days
The camps are crewed by family men
from safe and civilized villages
The glory days are a dwindling dream
as the logger becomes respectable

The sun goes down on those leather-tough times —
the logger that was has gone his way
leaving the pitted print of his boots —
the ghost of his song in the plundered draws.

Between The Sky And The Splinters

Sometimes at night when the mood is right
   a knock comes but nobody enters
except some old ghosts I knew on the coast
   between the sky and the splinters

There's mad Finn Billy   there's Grandaddy Tough
   there's panicky Tightline Flanders
there's Fullbore Dan and Marlinspike Stan
   between the sky and the splinters

I never heard men who could curse so well
   as those quarrelsome choker benders —
they were poets of oath in the undergrowth
   between the sky and the splinters

It was fog and blizzard and toughluck skies
   that curse back fire when it thunders
then spit down rain like a ruptured main
   between the sky and the splinters

But sometimes laughter honest and loud
   rings like coins from the minters —
the day turns glad and she ain't all bad
   between the sky and the splinters

The inkslinger's toting your money up
   it'll buy the king of all benders —
the thought comes sweet and you gulp it neat
   between the sky and the splinters

Who gives a damn when you've dropped your wad
in the till at the liquor vendors
that you'll limp back sore to sweat some more
between the sky and the splinters?

I meet them still in my loggingcamp dreams
those ornery sidehill mentors —
we laugh or curse for better or worse
between the sky and the splinters

But the game's gone bust   all the donkeys rust —
we've sold our youth to the vintners —
the last hill's crossed and the past lies lost
between the sky and the splinters.

The Ravens

Wherever it begins
on whatever cloudsoaked hill
torn by the whip of a tough man's sneer
humiliated
gestating poems and poison
crying tears they can't see
I'm still a rigging slave slandering God
wanting to quit when the wind spits water

They circle strange in the curdled sky
black messengers
bearing indecipherable messages
Oldtime loggers
named them soulbearers
where you go when you die
to wake feathered and swooping
your fat brain reduced
to a walnut of useful instinct
black wings slicing
through a universe of air
better than fools bent and cursing
on blasphemous hills

Bugs burrow
snakes crawl
ravens swoop

Cold on unknown mountains
I crack my barriers slowly
Time is only
amorphous mortar
holding the bricks apart
The cable I hold in my hand
was fashioned by slaves in other factories
This factory has no roof
Its walls are the world

I dream of death and ravens
sky and silence
the last log   takes me
My arms become feathered
I flap upward from blood
Ravens swoop
I swoop with them

Epilogue

Grapple Yarder
for Yvonne

Modern-day mountain stripper
it rattles from claim to claim
casting its steel claw across the slopes —
fishing for scattered logs with a three-man crew —
logs it took us ten men or more to harvest
with spar-trees and rattletrap donkeys long ago

But the years have galloped away —
I come as an onlooker now
riding a company truck up giddy roads
to stand among tourists watching the grapple duel
with a hung-up log in the bowl of a battered valley
whipping its lines like a man with a rod and reel

Snorting in diesel frustration
the yarder rocks back on its tracks —
clanks to a new location —
reefs and wrenches once more
but the stubborn full length fir declines to surrender —
they skin back a power-saw

The hooktender moves to his task —
we hear the rasp of the chain —
the long stick yields to the teeth —
once again the grapple yards —
we offer up a spontaneous round of applause
as the conquered fir comes jerking home in two parts

We wind down the breakneck road
above the Alberni Canal —
I feel the tugging of time —
a nostalgic pang for logging years long gone —
The ways have changed   the face of the woods has changed
but the old game goes on.

A Glossary of Logging Terms

A-Frame: Essentially a floating spar tree. Two raised logs were cabled together, with the high-lead blocks suspended from a lofty cross-brace. The whole business, including the donkey engine, rested on a giant raft. Used for yarding steep shorelines, this method of logging is virtually a thing of the past in BC, although it is still practiced in Alaska.

Back Line Stump: In high-lead logging, the haulback cable is run out into the brush, through two guide blocks and back to the machine. These guide blocks are hung on back line stumps, chosen and notched by the hooktender. The blocks are moved from stump to stump as the yarding progresses around the spar tree.

Backpack: Portable water pump worn like a packboard and used primarily for dousing spot fires in a burned-over area.

Bight: Used loosely, to be "in the bight" is to be in any risky logging situation. More specifically, it refers to the area within the curve of any diverted line. Since lines under tension have a tendency to straighten themselves, suddenly and without warning, it is a notoriously poor place to stand.

Block: A steel pulley used for guiding or diverting cables in the woods.

Bone-Dry Clothes: Before the development of tough, light rain gear, these garments were widely used in the woods. They consisted of two layers of canvas with a thin sheet of rubber between. The main drawback was their stiffness, which increased with age and led them to be referred to as "tin pants"and/or "tin coats." Hats were also made from this same material.

Boom: Logs in the water, sorted according to species and made up into sectioned rafts for towing to the mills.

Boom Man: The worker, quick on his feet and not averse to getting wet, who performs the foregoing function.

Boom Stick: A long log with an auger hole at either end, through which the boom chains are threaded. Strung out in series, they enclose the booming grounds and provide a basic framework for the booms themselves.

Bull Pen: An area enclosed by boom sticks into which unsorted logs are dumped.

Bull Block: The largest and the heaviest block used in the woods. Hangs up the spar tree as a guide for the main line.

Bull Team: Original log-moving method on the West Coast. Teams of up to a dozen oxen were yoked together to drag the timber out of the woods. It was rendered obsolete around 1905 with the development of the steam donkey.

Butt Rigging: A series of shackles and swivels to which the chokers are attached. It hangs between the eyes of the haul-back and main-line cables.

Camp Inspector: A short-stake artist or timber tramp. Seldom works more than a couple of weeks for any one outfit.

Cat: Caterpillar tractor, used both for bulldozing and, with the addition of an arch attachment, for hauling logs.

Cat Show: Logging area, usually not too steep, where it is more practical to use Cats with hauling arches to move the logs rather than the high-lead system.

Caulk Boots: Logger's traditional footgear since the Eastern river-driving days. Heavy-duty leather boots with spiked soles, to facilitate walking on logs both in and out of the water.

Chaser: Man who unhooks the logs at the spar tree. Job is now generally known as "landing man" and also involves bucking and stamping the logs, and sometimes setting the loading tongs that hoist them aboard the trucks.

Choker: A short length of steel cable with a ferrule on each end and a sliding bell fastener. One end is attached to the butt rigging. The other end is taken around the log and hooked into the bell, forming a slip noose. Thus throttled or "choked," the log is dragged to the spar tree. Two and even three chokers are used in a typical yarding setup, unless the country is unusually rough and the timber is very large.

Choker Hole: To effect the passage of the choker around the log, it is sometimes necessary to dig one of these. A favorite trick of playful hooktenders in times gone by was to send unsuspecting greenhorns in vain search of a sackful.

Choker Man: Lowest-paid job on a yarding crew, since the elimination of the whistlepunk. Novices usually start in this position and hook up logs under the direction of a rigging slinger.

Claim: General term for logging area, owned or under lease to a particular outfit.

Cold Deck: A pile of yarded logs around the base of a spar tree.

Crummy: Company truck or bus in which the logger is transported to and from his labours. Old army personnel carriers were widely used for this purpose during the 1950s.

Cultus: Coast Indian word meaning "bad" or "ill-omened."

D-8: A large heavy-duty Cat, widely used in the woods.

Diesel Rig: Logging truck or donkey powered by diesel fuel.

Donkey: Workhorse of the woods. A stationary engine set on a heavy wooden sled. Has evolved from primitive steam rigs to the compact diesel units of today. Generally has three winches- one each for the main line, haulback and straw line.

Donkey Puncher: The engineer who operates the foregoing machine.

Early Shift: A shift worked by loggers in very dry weather. Generally from 6:00 a.m. to 2:00 p.m., its purpose is to avoid the high fire hazard of late afternoon.

Faller: The shock troops of the woods, they cut down the timber ahead of the yarding crews. In the days of hand falling, this was a gruelling business indeed. It took great stamina to pull a crosscut saw all day, often balanced on a narrow springboard high above the ground. The development of the chainsaw has lightened this task considerably, but it is still highly dangerous work, fraught with many hazards. As a consequence, the fallers are the highest paid of the woods workers.

Fire Season: Throughout the Pacific Northwest, a period — usually from June to October — when danger of forest fire is most severe.

G Plane: A small aircraft used in fire-fighting operations to guide the cumbersome water bombers over their target areas.

Guthammer: Fixture of old-time cookhouses. Generally a steel triangle which the cook would rattle with a metal bar to signify mealtimes.

Guyline: One of several (generally six) bracing cables on a spar tree. On especially tall trees and on trackside trees — which were subject to greater strain because of the loading equipment — four or more additional guylines were used.

Gyppo: A small, independent logger or logging camp. The name drives from the fact that such outfits often went bankrupt, causing paycheques to bounce. Once the West Coast abounded with them, but rising costs and the imposition of a timber-quota system put most of them out of business by the end of the 1950s. Those gyppos that remain are invariable under contract to the big logging companies.

Hand Faller: Oldtime crosscut sawyer- frequently Scandinavian- who put the trees down the hard way.

Haulback Line: The secondary cable in a high-lead yarding

operation. Used to pull the butt rigging and the main line back out to the woods after each turn of logs is unhooked.

Heel Boom: A log-loading device. Essentially a giant wooden rack. It was suspended about thirty feet up a trackside spar tree and could be swung back and forth like a hinge. Logs to be loaded were hooked off-centre with steel tongs that hungdown from the boom. The short ends of the logs were lifted against a steel plate on the underside of the boom, pivoted or "heeled" completely off the ground and swung over the logging truck.

High-Lead: First used around 1911, this system became the most commonly used method for getting felled timber out of the woods. A spar tree sat in the centre of the area to be logged. The main function of the spar was to provide "lift" for the yarding cables, which ran through two large lead blocks near the top of the tree and out into the woods. Without "lift," the incoming logs tended to become fouled or "hung up" behind stumps and other obstacles. The loggers worked around the spar tree in a system of roads like the spokes of a wheel. The high-lead system evolved from the mast rigging used in sailing ships.

High-Notched Stumps: Ghostly monuments to a hardier breed, they are found throughout the old logging areas of the Pacific Northwest. The notches are the springboard holes of early fallers, who used this method to climb above the butt swell of the huge trees.

High Rigger: The steeplejack of the woods. He did the tree-topping and rigged up the spar trees, hanging the high-lead blocks and guylines, etc. Many of the early high riggers were former seamen, accustomed to clambering around in the shrouds of windjammers.

Hooktender: The undisputed boss of the yarding unit or "side," he took orders only from the side rod or superintendent. In small gyppo camps, the hooktender usually did the high-rigging chores as well.

Landing: The area around the base of a spar tree where the logs are landed.

Loading Pot: A small gas donkey used to operate the heel boom in the loading process.

Locie Show: Operation using locomotives instead of trucks for log-hauling.

Log Count: The number of logs yarded to the landing in any one shift.

Main Line: The heavy cable that pulls the logs to the spar tree.

Mancatcher: A shill for the Vancouver logging agencies. His job was to hang about the Skidroad pubs and induce idle loggers to accept work at one of his employer's camps — generally a substandard operation.

Molly Hogan: A single strand of six-strand cable, wound several times around itself and locking into its own lay to form a strong several-stranded ring. Used to join two cable eyes or in place of a cotter key in blocks.

Peavey: Heavy-handled woods tool with a spike point and free-swinging hook, used for rolling logs. Named after its inventor, George Peavey, a legendary Eastern lumberjack.

Pike Pole: Primary tool of boom men in the days before modern dozer boats. Long pole, of wood or aluminum, with a pike-tipped end that can both push and pull. In pre-mechanical times, log-booms were "stowed" or put together by gangs of men using these implements.

Pulling Levers: Operating a loading donkey.

Raised Tree: On a setting where there was no suitable standing tree to be topped for a spar, it was necessary to raise one. This was done with the yarding donkey, using a system of block purchases and a gin pole — or intermediary tree — to provide lift.

Rigging Crew: The various members of the yarding unit, from the whistlepunk to the hooktender.

Rigging Slinger: Essentially a strawboss, second-in-command to the hooktender. He picks out the logs for the chokermen to set, and shouts the signals to the whistlepunk.

Road Line: The segment of the logging area presently being yarded.

Setting: The entire area being worked by a yarding unit.

Show: Can mean the same as "setting" but generally refers to the whole logging operation, including the camp.

Side: One yarding unit in a large camp.

Side Rod: General woods foreman in charge of the "sides."

Sidewinding Log: If a small or medium-sized log runs up against a stump in the yarding process, it can pivot violently sideways. It is advisable to be well clear when this occurs.

Sinker: Very heavy log — usually hemlock — that will barely float. Often becomes that bane of the boat men the deadhead, floating straight up and down in the water with only a small portion visible.

Skidroad: Originally meant greased corduroy road down which logs were hauled by oxen or horses. Now used in reference to seamier areas of cities such as Vancouver and Seattle, where loggers were wont to squander their hard-come-by cash. The term "skidrow," widely used by the uninformed, is a corruption.

Skyline: Heavy cable hung between two spar trees, along which a two-wheeled carriage rode. It provided additional lift for the logs in extremely rough country. There were many variations of this system, which is seldom used anymore.

Slash: A logged-over area. As a verb, it means to cut line for a survey crew.

Slash Fire: A deliberate fire set on a logged-over ground to burn up potentially fire-hazardous debris.

Snare: Another term for a choker.

Snoose: Powdered chewing tobacco, widely used by the old-time loggers.

Spar Tree: The heart of a high-lead logging operation. Mostly replaced in modern-day logging by portable steel-spar units.

Stagged-Off Pants: Loggers generally bucked their jeans off about halfway up the calf to facilitate movement and prevent tearing.

Steam Rig: Steam-powered donkey engine of early high-lead days.

Straw Line: Light utility cable, used for stringing the heavier lines.

Suicide Show: A particularly dangerous logging claim.

Tame Ape: Along with brush ape, timber beast and rangitang, a term for rigging men or loggers in general.

Tie-Up Lines: Cables used to anchor a yarding donkey or to secure the base of a spar tree in a raising operation.

Topping: Cutting the top off a standing tree to ready it for use as a spar. It was occasionally done with dynamite, but mostly with axes and saws.

Whistlepunk: The signalman on a rigging crew. Job was usually done by very young boys or very old men — since it involved little physical work. The development of electronic belt-whistles has rendered this job obsolete.

Printed and bound
in Boucherville, Quebec, Canada by
MARC VEILLEUX IMPRIMEUR INC.
in July, 1999